# 彩衣笛手

# The Pied Piper

retold by Henriette Barkow
illustrated by Roland Dry

Chinese translation by Sylvia Denham

mantra

有些人相信這故事是真的，有些人卻不以爲然，不過無論是真是假，我都會將
故事說給你聽。

在很多年以前的古代時期，有一個名叫漢密林的市鎮，它只是一個普通的市鎮，
住著普通的人，就好像你和我一樣。
有一年，市鎮受到**老鼠**侵襲，有大隻的老鼠、細小的老鼠、肥老鼠和瘦老鼠，
不管你往那裏望，你都會見到**老鼠**！

Some people believe this story is true, and others that it is not. But either way this story
I will tell to you.

    Many years ago, in the days of old, there was a town called Hamelin. It was an
ordinary town, with ordinary people just like you and me.
    One year the town had an invasion of RATS. There were big rats and small rats, fat
rats and thin rats. Wherever you looked there were RATS!

你可以想像到市鎮的居民十分不安，他們衝進市鎮的會堂，並要求市長採取行動。
「你們想我做什麼？」他大聲叫道，「我不是一個捕鼠者啊！」

As you can imagine, the people of the town were very upset. They stormed
to the town hall and demanded that the mayor do something.
"What do you expect me to do?" he shouted. "I'm not a rat catcher!"

就在此時，一個陌生人出現，他穿著奇異的衣服，手裏拿著一根笛子。群眾盯著這陌生人，就好像一般人通常盯著陌生人一樣，但他毫不動容。

At that very moment a stranger appeared, wearing the most unusual clothes and holding a pipe in his hand. The crowd stared at the stranger, the way that people often stare at strangers, but that didn't bother him.

那陌生人一直走到市長面前介紹自己，「他們稱我爲彩衣笛手，如果你給我二十
枚金塊，我會將你所有的老鼠趕走。」
這對市長來說就好像動聽的音樂，「如果你真的能做到你所說的，我將會樂於支
付你，」他回答道。

The stranger walked straight up to the mayor and introduced himself. "They call me the
Pied Piper and if you pay me twenty pieces of gold I will take all your rats away."
Well this was music to the mayor's ears. "If you can truly do what you say, I shall be more
than happy to pay you," he replied.

市鎮的居民等著，看看這名為彩衣笛手的人是否真的能趕走所有老鼠 - 大隻的老鼠、細小的老鼠、年幼的老鼠和老的老鼠呢？

The town's people waited and watched. Could this so called Pied Piper really get rid of all the rats - the big rats and the small rats, the young rats and the old rats?

彩衣笛手慢慢地開始吹奏他的笛子，令人難以致信的事情便跟著
發生，老鼠從每一個角落和隙縫處走到街上，牠們受到音樂的魔
力所吸引，跟著笛手後面走。

The Pied Piper slowly started to play his pipe and an unbelievable
thing happened. From every nook and cranny the rats poured out onto
the street, and under the spell of the music, they followed the piper.

牠們跟著他走出漢密林市，向著威悉河去，到了河邊，笛手將音調改變，老鼠隨著悲傷哀悼的調子自動跳進冰冷的河水，遭河水淹沒。

They followed him out of Hamelin town to the river Weser. Here, the Pied Piper changed his tune and with a mournful wailing, the rats threw themselves into the icy water and drowned.

漢密林的市長是一個貪心的人，他根本沒有準備給那陌生人任何酬勞，當彩衣笛手到來要求他應得的金塊時，市長一邊笑一邊搖頭，「現在老鼠都走掉了，我爲什麼要給你任何東西？」他罵道。

Now the mayor of Hamelin was a greedy man, and he wasn't going to give any money to a stranger. When the Pied Piper came and demanded his pieces of gold the mayor laughed and shook his head. "Now that the rats are gone why should I give you anything?" he snarled.

市鎮的居民只是站著聽，即使明知市長是錯的，他們也不去支持笛手，默不作聲，站著不理。

The people stood and listened. They didn't stand up for the piper, even though they knew that their mayor was wrong. They didn't say a word.

「再想清楚啊，市長！」笛手警告他，「如果你不付金塊，
我便令這市鎮受到你難以想像的折磨。」
市長想不出有什麼比老鼠還差，於是他一邊大聲叫一邊走
離會堂，「我永遠也不會支付你的！」

"Think again, mayor!" the piper warned. "If you don't pay,
then I will make this town suffer more than you can ever
imagine."
    Well the mayor couldn't think of anything worse than
the rats and so he stomped off shouting:
"I WILL NEVER PAY YOU!"

就在那天下午，當各人忙於重整市鎮時，彩衣服笛手站在市鎮的廣
場上，他慢慢地將笛子提到唇邊，吹奏出一首沒有字句能形容的調子，

That very afternoon, while the people were busy repairing their
town, the Pied Piper stood in the town square. Slowly he lifted the
pipe to his lips, and played a tune that no words could describe.

當每一個音調奏出時，都有越來越多
的兒童出現，隨著音樂跳舞和唱歌。

With each new note more and more children appeared,
and danced and sang to the music.

彩衣笛手轉身走出市鎮，吹奏著他的笛子，
所有的兒童受到他的音樂的魔力所 及引都跟著他走。

The Pied Piper turned and walked out of the town playing his pipe and all the children followed, caught under the spell of his music.

他們跟著音樂的旋律跳舞和唱歌，往山上走去，
當他們走到盡頭時，一度門在他們面前打開，

Up the hill they danced and sang to the rhythm of the tune. When it
looked like they could go no further, a door opened before them.

所有孩子一個一個的跟著彩衣笛手走近山野深處，永不回來，
只有一個小孩趕不上其他的孩子而沒有進入深山。

One by one the children followed the Pied Piper into the heart of
the hill forever. All except one, who could not keep up with the others.

當這小孩回到市鎮時，魔力就好像被毀破一樣，他告訴各人他
經歷的情況，他們都盯著他，不能相信發生的事情。
他們呼喚他們的孩子，但他們永遠都不會再見到他們的孩子了。

When the little boy returned to the town it was as if a spell had been broken.
The people stared at him in disbelief when he told them what had happened.
They called and cried for their children, but they never saw them again.

# Key Words

| | |
|---|---|
| town | 市鎮 |
| people | 市民 |
| rats | 老鼠 |
| town hall | 市鎮會堂 |
| mayor | 市長 |
| rat catcher | 捕鼠者 |
| stranger | 陌生人 |
| clothes | 衣服 |
| pipe | 笛子 |
| crowd | 群眾 |
| pied piper | 彩衣笛手 |
| twenty | 二十 |
| pieces of gold | 金塊 |

# 主要生字詞語

| | |
|---|---|
| music | 音樂 |
| playing | 吹奏 |
| river | 河 |
| greedy | 貪心 |
| money | 金錢 |
| suffer | 折磨 |
| children | 兒童 |
| danced | 跳舞 |
| sang | 唱歌 |
| rhythm | 旋律 |
| tune | 調子 |
| hill | 山 |
| spell | 魔力 |

彩衣笛手的傳奇來自德國的漢密林市 [Hameln, Germany]，故事發生於 1284 年。
如果你想知道更多有關這傳說的資料，漢密林市有一個英語的網址：

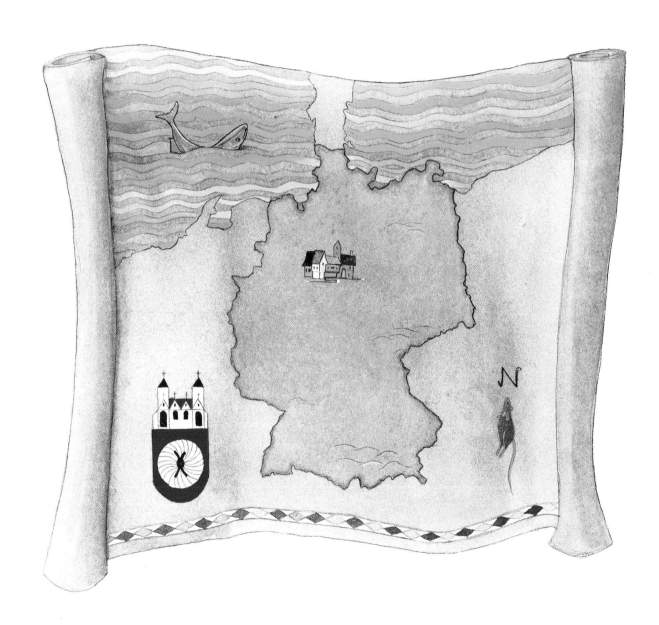

The legend of the Pied Piper originates from events that took place in the town of Hameln in Germany. The story dates back to 1284. If you would like more information the town of Hameln has an excellent website in English: http://www.hameln.com/englis

If you've enjoyed this bilingual story in Chinese & English look out for other
Mantra titles in Chinese & English

## Folk stories in Mantra's World Tales Series

Buri and the Marrow- an Indian folk story
Buskers of Bremen - adapted from the Brothers Grimm
Don't Cry Sly - adapted from Aesop's Fables
Dragon's Tears - a Chinese folk story
The Giant Turnip - a Russian folk story
Goldilocks and the Three Bears
Jack and the Beanstalk - an English folk story
Not Again Red Riding Hood
The Pied Piper - a German legend
Three Billy Goats Gruff - a Scandinavian folk story

## Mantra's Contemporary Story Series

Alfie's Angels
Flash Bang Wheee!
Lima's Red Hot Chilli
Mei Ling's Hiccups
Sam's First Day
The Swirling Hijaab
That's My Mum
The Wibbly Wobbly Tooth

## Myths and Legends in Mantra's World Heritage Series

Beowulf - an Anglo Saxon Epic
The Children of Lir - a Celtic Myth
Hanuman's Challenge - an Indian Myth
Pandora's Box - a Greek Myth

## Mantra's Classic Story Series

Handa's Surprise
Splash!
The Very Hungry Caterpillar
Walking Through the Jungle
We're going on a Bear Hunt
What shall we do with the Boo Hoo Baby?

Many of the above books are also available on audio CD. To see the full range of Mantra's resources
do visit our website at www.mantralingua.com